Kissing

The
complete Guide

Tamar Schreibman

Kissing
The complete Guide

Tamar Schreibman

Aladdin Paperbacks
New York London Toronto Sydney Singapore

First Aladdin Paperbacks edition January 2000

Copyright © 2000 by Tamar Schreibman

Aladdin Paperbacks
An imprint of Simon & Schuster
Children's Publishing Division
1230 Avenue of the Americas
New York, NY 10020

Designed by Steve Scott
The text for this book was set in Versaille
Printed and bound in the United States of America

2 4 6 8 10 9 7 5 3

Library of Congress Cataloging-in-Publication Data
Schreibman, Tamar.
Kissing : the complete guide / by Tamar Schreibman.
— 1st Aladdin Paperbacks ed.
p.   cm.
Summary: Explains what kissing is, the origins of the custom, how to do it, what to expect, quotes, a quiz on kissing, and more.
ISBN 0-689-83329-6
[1. Kissing—Juvenile literature. 2. Kissing.]
I. Title.
GT2640.S34   394'21
99-54387
CIP AC

Introduction

I have a confession to make: I turned sweet sixteen without ever having been kissed. By the time that momentous birthday rolled around, all my friends had already had their first kisses (and many of them their second and third and fourth). But I had somehow managed to make it through school dances, parties where everyone else played spin the bottle, summer camp mixers, and even a first boyfriend without a real kiss. It's not that I still thought boys had cooties. In fact, I had been plagued for years by enormous crushes on different boys, and I had spent hours and hours speculating about what my first kiss would be like, who it would be with, and how in the world would it ever happen to me. I pretty much figured that if I had made it to this point kiss-less, I was doomed for a life without kisses.

But about midway through that sixteenth year, everything changed for me. A boy I had been crushing on for over a year finally asked me out, and before I knew it I was sitting next to him on my mom's beige corduroy couch, sneaking my first kiss. I was finally in on the big secret, part of the club! I was absolutely thrilled that I had kissed a boy in general, and kissing him made me like this boy in particular even more. Even though we didn't ride off into the sunset together, that kiss on the corduroy couch was just the beginning. My initiation into the world of kissing had made me bolder and more confident. I was nervous and excited but no longer paralyzed by the thought of kissing. I got new boyfriends, kissed them, had my heart broken, kissed more boys, got more boyfriends, and haven't stopped kissing since.

That's the amazing thing about kissing. It never gets boring. No matter how old you are or how many people you've kissed, each time you kiss someone new, your heart dances a little jig, your stomach feels queasy, and everything around you seems a little different. And it's not just the first kiss. When you really like someone, kissing him is always a treat, even if you and he have been smooching for years.

Kissing is totally natural, but if you've never locked lips, it is hard to imagine that you will ever be able to figure out what to do when that special somebody leans in for the kill (Where do you put your nose? Should you close your eyes? What are you going to do with your arms? Should you open your mouth?). It's even more impossible to imagine how you will ever be brave enough to initiate a kiss yourself. This book is devoted entirely to kissing. (If you want to know more about the other stuff, you'll need to find a different book.) It will not only give you answers to your nagging questions about what to do, but will also tell you things about kissing that even the most experienced kisser might not know, or even think to ask.

Chapter 1
Is a Kiss Just a Kiss?

Kiss: "to touch with the lips, especially as a mark of affection or greeting . . . to touch gently or lightly . . . to salute or caress one another with the lips"— Merriam-Webster's Collegiate Dictionary, Tenth Edition.

Most people don't need to look up the word "kiss" in the dictionary to understand what it means. But there are actually several layers of meaning to this endlessly fascinating word.

The first part of the definition, "to touch with the lips, especially as a mark of affection or greeting," is nothing new to any of us. This kind of kissing is the most normal thing in the world, something we've all done a million times, maybe even on a daily basis. Since the moment we were born we have been the regular recipients of these sweet, affectionate kisses. When we were little we were showered with kisses at bedtime when our parents tucked us in to say good night, or after we fell down and scraped our knees. These kisses made us feel warm, comforted, and safe. Our foreheads, our cheeks, our lips, our knees, our noses, our tummies, and even the bottoms of our feet have been kissed in this first sense of the word. We have not simply accepted these kisses; we have learned how to return them as well.

This first definition, of course, also includes the often-dreaded kiss-on-the-cheek greeting from random adults like parents' friends or distant aunts. These kisses can be nice, but they can also be annoying when accompanied by a pinch on the cheek and a comment about how much we've grown. They have the tendency to make us shy, embarrassed, or even grossed out (especially if the kisser seems really old, gives big, wet, sloppy kisses, or looks like she's going to leave lipstick on our faces).

The second part of the definition, "to touch gently or lightly," seems at first glance like the least interesting. A person who has a tiny bit of color from the sun may be described, for example, as "sun-kissed." Or, when you're sitting in class and some smart-aleck boy throws a paper airplane, it might brush or "kiss" your arm. But this definition actually sheds light on how powerful a kiss can be. While it describes a touch so light that it can barely be felt, it also describes a touch that leaves one or both of the parties a little bit different. (The sun's kiss leaves you slightly browner; by kissing your arm, the airplane changes directions or stops altogether.)

This concept of a kiss's extraordinary power can be applied to the third and, many would say, the most delicious definition of kissing: "to salute or caress one another with the lips." This kiss is in a league all of its own. Maybe you or some of your friends or classmates have kissed this way. You've definitely seen people kiss like this on TV or at the movies. Chances are if you've ever seen your parents kissing each other this way, you've probably begged them to stop. Your big sister might have already kissed someone this way, and even though it's hard to imagine, your grandparents, aunts and uncles, cafeteria ladies, and teachers have, too.

Different Kinds of Kisses

Osculum—Latin for "social kiss"

Basium—Latin for "romantic kiss"

Suavium—Latin for "deep kiss" (what Americans call a French kiss)

French kiss—Passionate kissing, where both partners use their tongues as well as their lips. This term entered the English vocabulary in 1923 because Americans thought of French people as very sexy. (The French, however, don't use this term. They call this kind of kiss a "tongue kiss" or a "soul kiss."

Butterfly kiss—Kissing with your eyelashes by fluttering your lids against a cheek.

Maraichinage kiss—Tongues touch lightly and then quickly pull away—like a frog. Named after the Maraichins, inhabitants of Brittany in France, who are said to kiss this way for hours.

Hershey's (chocolate) Kisses

And what might be even harder to believe if you are still a novice is that at some point in your life you, too, will probably experience many kisses like this. But don't freak out if the thought isn't entirely appealing: There is no need to smooch before you're ready.

Kissing is a form of communication; it's a way to show that you really like someone. It is natural, but it's not automatic. You don't need to study in order to be a good kisser, but a little research can be fun and might even come in handy someday.

Chapter 2
Kiss-Story
(A Brief History of Kissing)

You might think it looks appealing when Monica and Chandler share one of their short and sweet, yet meaningful kisses. But if you have ever seen a kiss in a movie (think the Austin Powers movies or *Titanic*) that is long, intense, and tongue-heavy, it has probably made you wonder not only *why do they kiss for so long?* and *how can that be fun?* but *who ever thought of kissing in the first place?* Why don't people, for example, just give each other the thumbs-up sign or wink to demonstrate their affection, and leave it at that?

Let's begin by examining the origins of the ordinary social kiss. We know that people have been kissing for a long time as a way to greet each other. It is believed that the ancient Romans were the ones who started this. They greeted friends, family, and even acquaintances with kisses on the cheek, and showed respect to their leaders by kissing their robes and rings.

In the Middle Ages in Europe (around A.D. 500–1500), rank determined where you would kiss someone when saying hello. The lower you were on the totem pole, the farther from the face you had to kiss—you'd kiss peers on the mouth (imagine doing that at school!); kiss those whose status was above you on the hand; kiss those even higher than that on the knee; and as for the highest class (mostly religious figures), you kissed them on the foot. (That's where the phrase "I kiss the ground you walk on" comes from.)

Friendly kissing remained popular throughout Europe after the Middle Ages ended. In England during the Renaissance (which lasted into the seventeenth century), hosts would welcome guests by encouraging them to kiss each family member on the lips. But you still had to be careful whom you kissed, because it was illegal to kiss someone in a class above you. When the Great Plague swept through Europe, people's enthusiasm for kissing waned, and when it struck

A Kiss Around the World

Italian: *bacio* (sounds like BAH-cho)

German: *küsse* (sounds like koo-sa)

Hebrew: *na'shikah* (sounds like nuh-shee-ka)

Hungarian: *csók* (sounds like choke)

Greek: *filie* (sounds like fee-LEE)

Russian: *potselui* (sounds like pot-sell-oo-wee)

Hindi: *chummi* (sounds like choo-me)

Spanish: *beso* (sounds like bay-so)

French: *un baiser* (sounds like bes-ay)

Since French is such a famously romantic language, here are a few more French kissing terms: *embrasse-moi* means "kiss me." A nice way to sign off at the end of a letter is *grosses bisous* (literally, "big kisses").

Korean: *boh-boh*

Burmese: *hmway-hmway* (means, literally, "sweet smell")

England in 1665, people there stopped kissing altogether for years, for fear of catching the deadly disease.

The social peck was also popular in France, where King Louis XIII (1601–43) was famous for kissing every woman in Normandy. People eventually started to greet each other with kisses on the hands (probably out of fear of spreading germs), and the hand kiss over time evolved into the even more sanitary handshake.

Obviously the social kiss made a comeback and is still alive and well in many parts of the modern world. But when did people start to make kissing so mushy and romantic? The first evidence of this type of kiss was actually found on pottery in Peru from around 200 B.C., and some say the first romantic kiss was exchanged between lovers as long ago as 1500 B.C. in India.

But maybe the more important question is *why* did people start swapping spit to show they cared about each other? There are a lot of wacky theories on how smooching became so popular, and no one knows which, if any, is accurate.

Some say it all started before there was baby food, when mothers had to chew food first to make it soft enough for their babies to eat it. To transfer it from her own mouth to that of her baby, she would press her lips against her child's, and this eventually evolved into an adult form of affection (pretty gross, huh?).

Have you ever noticed that your dog likes to lick your skin, especially on hot days? One theory is that people in the Stone Age realized that salt cools you down on hot days, and they also found that licking each other was an easy way to get salt. Somehow, this theory goes, that turned into kissing.

Others claim that ancient religions believed that breath held the soul, and therefore had a magic power. People would exchange breath (through kissing) for religious purposes. This is also an explanation for the ritual of a bride and groom kissing after they exchange vows.

Eskimos, Laplanders, and Polynesians all kiss by rubbing each other's noses together. Some believe this is rooted in the animal instinct to smell each other when they see each other (again, think of dogs).

And some say kissing evolved from our instinct to breast-feed. According to this theory, kissing is just a way to satisfy this natural urge to do something with our mouths.

The Power of the Kiss

A kiss is a powerful thing. It has healing powers: You kiss and make up after a fight; mothers kiss their children's scrapes and cuts to make them feel better. If you've ever seen a Mafia movie, there's the kiss on the lips from the hit man before the mobster gets killed. There's also the kiss of death that Judas gave Jesus before he betrayed him. In the Middle Ages, people who couldn't read or write would sign legal contracts by making an "X" and then kissing it to show that they intended to honor it. (That's how "XX" became short-hand for a kiss.)

Chapter 3

The First Kiss

Overcoming Nervousness

If you think there's a lot of pressure when it comes to a first kiss, consider this: In the Middle Ages in Italy, if a man kissed a woman in public, he was obligated to marry her. So don't freak out too much; a first kiss is thrilling, dramatic, and anxiety-producing, but your whole life isn't riding on it. You will have time to practice until you get it just right.

Fear of Rejection

A common and understandable fear is that your desire to kiss someone is not mutual. The problem is, a lot of the time the girl is thinking, *when is he going to kiss me?* and the guy is thinking, *should I kiss her?* Not many people are brave (or thick-skulled) enough to try to kiss someone who doesn't show any interest, so here are some clear signs to watch for (or to send out) that scream, "Kiss me, you fool!" Don't worry if you've missed a ton of opportunities already—even experienced kissers miss them all the time!

Green-Light Signs
(Otherwise Known as Flirting)

tons of eye contact
big smiles and lots of laughs
paying a lot of attention to each other
standing or sitting close together
touching each other's arms in the middle
    of the conversation, usually while
    making a point
paying compliments
inviting to each other's places
playing with hair or clothing (girls tend
    to do this more than boys)

Making the Move

So you are pretty sure that he would like to kiss you, too. But how in the world do you get from the flirting to the kissing? Lots of girls wait for the guy to kiss them, but if you like a boy, it's okay to kiss him first. Remember, there are a lot of unkissed frogs out there yearning to become princes. In fact, a recent *YM* poll found that 61 percent of their female readers had initiated a kiss. If he seems interested, make some physical contact: Stand closer; touch him while you're talking; gaze directly into his eyes; perhaps glance at his lips now and then, as well. If he hasn't made the move by now, why not give it a try? If you're still worried about rejection, pause briefly while you're moving in, before touching his lips, to see if he moves forward to meet yours. (Yet another approach is to ask if it's okay to kiss him. Not all people like to be asked first, because it doesn't seem confident, while others find it touching and polite.)

A popular and less scary method of scoring a first kiss is through games, often played in groups.

Kissing Games

Spin the bottle: Players sit in a circle and take turns spinning an empty soda bottle. The person spinning then has to kiss whomever the bottle is pointing to when it stops.

The hugging game: Often played on dance floors, this game is like musical chairs, but when the music stops, instead of trying to find a chair to sit in, the girls have to find a boy to kiss. Here's how it works: The guys stand in a circle, shoulder to shoulder, and the girls run around until the music stops. That's when they have to run up to a guy and kiss (or hug) him. If more than one girl wants to kiss the same guy, the first one to stand next to him wins. This means she gets to kiss him, and stay in the game.

Truth or dare: Participants choose whether they want to take a dare, or promise to tell the truth when asked a question. For example: If Susie chooses truth, she will have to answer a question like, "Have you ever kissed a boy?" If she chooses dare, she might have to kiss Charlie.

Post office: One person plays postman or postwoman, and then someone tells one of the others that he or she has "mail." When that person goes to pick up the mail, he or she gets a kiss from the postman or postwoman instead of a letter.

Seven minutes in heaven: Often an off-shoot of spin the bottle, but instead of kissing in front of everyone, the "couple" has to go into a private area for an allotted period of time (which usually ends up being less than seven minutes).

Performance Anxiety

In many ways your first kiss is a landmark event. From now on you may look at members of the opposite sex in a whole new light—as potential kissing partners—and you will probably never go back. . . .

If you've never kissed before, there's a lot to wonder about. How do you know what to do? How will you know if you're going to be the world's worst kisser? What if you hate it? How will you know when to stop, and what to do or say afterward?

Whether you've kissed a hundred

times or never before, kissing someone new for the first time is a nerve-racking experience. One thing to remember is that there are no rules. There are many kinds of kisses, and everyone likes to kiss a little differently. When you kiss someone new, it might be perfect or it might take a while for the two of you to discover—together—what works best.

What to Expect

When you sense that a kiss is in your very near future, your heart might start pounding, you'll feel butterflies in your stomach, and your palms might begin to sweat. You might not be able to think of anything to say. (Don't worry, because if he's busy working up the courage to kiss you, he is probably too nervous to be listening to what you're saying, anyway.) You might wonder how, until this very moment, you had never noticed how cute those freckles on his nose are. Then, before you know it, you're kissing. All those questions that have been running through your mind up until now (Where do I put my nose? How long will it last?

Do I keep my eyes closed the whole time? Where do I put my arms? Is my breath okay? What will I say when it's over?) will probably vanish, and you'll just feel like melting. You won't be able to tell where his mouth ends and yours begins. Your sense of time may be distorted, and if you're standing you might feel dizzy and your legs might feel like jelly.

All of this is part of the excitement, so don't worry. Just try to enjoy it, but if you don't, you're not a total weirdo. In fact, a recent poll found that a lot of adults worried so much about how they were kissing, they didn't enjoy their first kiss. Thirty-eight percent of adults surveyed said the moment was spoiled because they were concentrating on their kissing technique instead of enjoying the kiss, and twenty-seven percent regret their first kiss because they wish they had kissed somebody else. (They should just be thankful that they didn't live in Italy in the Middle Ages; otherwise, they'd regret kissing the wrong person a whole lot more!) Five percent are bummed they didn't open their eyes, and two percent wish they had. This all goes to show you that you'll figure it out as you go along—and if this one isn't perfect, don't worry, because the kisses are going to get less stressful, and better and better and better.

Kissing Expressions

Kiss my grits.
kiss and tell
sweet sixteen and never been kissed
kissing cousins
Kiss me, you fool.
sealed with a kiss
stealing a kiss
shower with kisses
I kiss the ground you walk on.
Give me some sugar. (used in the South, when asking for a kiss)

Chapter 4

Memories of First Kisses

The moment occurs in many different ways. Some first kisses are meaningful, some are part of a game, some are planned, some are spontaneous, some are huge surprises, some can be seen coming from miles away, some are quick pecks, some are long and languorous, some are awesome, and some are repulsive. The one thing that almost every first kiss has in common is that it will be remembered forever.

Straightforward Smooches

A Walk in the Woods

My first real kiss was in eighth grade with my boyfriend, Paul, who was adorable (even my mom loved him). We went skating one Saturday and walked home by ourselves. We took the long way and then we cut through the woods and made out. It started as a series of kisses, and the pauses between them became fewer and fewer until they morphed into one long one. We sat on a rock. It was really uncomfortable because it was making a pointy indentation in my butt, but I didn't care at all. I was in heaven.

—Diana, Boston, Massachusetts

First Base at a Baseball Game

My first kiss was in sixth grade. I'd had a boyfriend the year before, but we broke up because I wouldn't kiss him. I was scared, plus I didn't want to be the first one of my friends to kiss. But then about six months later, all of my friends had kissed and I hadn't. Suddenly I was curious. I ended up "going together" with this boy a grade below me. A group of us went to a baseball game together and stood in the back by the concessions. I knew we were gonna kiss that night because baseball games were the place everyone always ended up kissing. We didn't watch the game; we just talked and flirted. The two of us walked away, holding hands, and went behind the bathroom where no one would see us. We were both really embarrassed that everyone knew what we were doing. We were very awkward; we had our arms stiffly around each other's waists. It was a short kiss. My heart was beating really loud, and I was worried he would notice. He smiled at me right after the kiss, and then, I remember, my heart kind of melted. When we walked back, everyone was asking if we had kissed and we said yes and then we went back to hanging out. We broke up a week later, but I was just psyched that I had kissed a boy.

—Barbara, Memphis, Tennessee

Seeing Red

I was very self-conscious about my appearance in elementary school because I had really crooked teeth. In eighth grade I had to have massive oral surgery, and then I waited months to heal, and then I got my braces (which I wore for three years). I met the guy who kissed me a few weeks after I'd had my braces put on and, having basically consumed nothing but liquids for the better part of a year, couldn't imagine doing anything with my mouth like kissing. His name was Eddie, and his family lived in the small town in northern Michigan, where my family spends weekends in the summertime. He was a couple of years older, and sort of a bad boy, and really cute.

So we were hanging out one day, and he'd come over, and then we left my house and we were going to take a walk. I remember walking along with this feeling that he was planning to kiss me, but really in total disbelief that a boy would ever want to kiss me. And then he just stopped me and gave me a smooch, braces and all. It wasn't very big or wet or anything, just a little kiss. I'm pretty sure I forgot to kiss back and just stood there smiling; I'm also pretty sure I kept my eyes wide open, because the color of his red football jersey is still burned on my brain.   —Carole, Oscoda, Michigan

A Perfect Gentleman

My first kiss happened on a school trip to Boston in eighth grade. I went to an all girls' school, and they gave us a special treat by letting us stay at an all boys' school rather than a hotel. We were housed in the infirmary, since all the dorms were occupied by the boys. The boys' school threw us a welcoming dance on our first night.

It was dark, and there were some spinning lights, and bowls of cheese curls that the girls didn't touch and the boys were gobbling down as they jostled each other, checking us out. Finally the music got going. We pretty much kept to ourselves, dancing in protective circles, occasionally glancing over our shoulders at the boys and flipping our hair. But then a slow song came on, and we all scurried off the floor in a giggling huddle.

All of a sudden I saw a boy striding boldly across the almost-empty dance floor, seemingly headed right toward me. He came over and held out his hand and asked if I wanted to dance. I had never seen a boy so formal before—the guys who had asked my friends to dance had kind of shuffled their feet and shoved their hands in their pockets, ducking their heads. So I took his hand and followed him out onto the dance floor. I put my arms around his neck, and he put his on my waist, and we kind of moved back and forth, turning every once in a while, the way you were supposed to slow dance. I could smell the cheese curls on his breath and feel his skin through his shirt. We ran through the customary slow-dancing, getting-to-know-you topics: names, favorite music, pets and siblings, homes. The lights spun around us, and I imagined all the other girls watching me, one of the privileged few who had been selected for slow dancing.

After the dance was over, Rich suggested we go for a walk outside. We slipped out the door, and I felt so tall and sophisticated, as if now I were above all the junior high school dance stuff and I had someone real to go off into the night with. He walked me to the door of the infirmary, and then we paused and he asked if he could come up. But at the top of the stairs, a wooden bench had been erected across the hallway, and a sign in turquoise crayon was taped to it: NO BOYS BEYOND THIS POINT. We turned to each other awkwardly, now that there was nowhere farther to go. "Well," I began. "I guess I have to go here."

"Yeah," he said, and now he shuffled from foot to foot and tugged down his tie. He considered the door to the stairwell, then turned abruptly back toward me and said quickly, as if afraid he would lose courage, "So can I give you a good-night kiss?"

"I guess so," I said. I always pretended to be less enthusiastic than I was. It was one of my tricks. He turned to me and put his arms around my waist, just as when we were dancing, and I put my arms around his neck. We paused with our faces close to each other, breathing. Now his breath smelled like nothing, like the dew on the grass, with an after-scent of Pepsi carbonation. He leaned in and pressed his lips to mine. I wasn't sure if I was kissing him back or not, but I didn't remove mine from under his. We stayed pressed together for approximately six seconds, I figured. We didn't hug each other. Then we came apart. We were silent for a moment, looking at our feet.

"You know," he said, "that was my first kiss."

"Mine too," I admitted shyly.

—Caitlin, Brooklyn, New York

Different Words used to Describe Kissing

first base
neck
make out
scam
get together with
peck
French
mash
canoodle (British)
snoggle (British)
fool around
smooch
hook up with
tongue wrestle
lock lips

Playing Games

Truth or Dare

I was in sixth grade. His last name was a mouthful and included the letters "s-p-a-z," so you can imagine what his nickname was. But I liked him. The sixth graders were in charge of walking kindergartners up the path toward school, and he requested that we walk next to each other. I was thrilled and considered him my boyfriend after that. One time we were at my house, and somehow I pulled off playing a game of truth or dare without the watchful eye of my parents. We were sitting on my parents' couch stiffly asking each other innocent questions. I finally dared him to kiss me on the cheek, and he took me up on it but not without giggling and hemming and hawing. Afterward I was stoked that I had had my first kiss.   —Lynn, Wilmette, Illinois

Spin the Bottle

I was in seventh grade, at a party out in the driveway at my house. There were about eight of us, and we decided to play spin the bottle. One of my guy friends spun the bottle, and it landed on me. I was lukewarm about him; he was sweet, but not totally cute (but not gross, either). Most of us hadn't kissed before. The point of the game was for us all to French kiss, but we didn't know what to do, so we were frozen. Our kiss was something in between a French kiss and a peck. It was not wholly unpleasant, but it took another kissing experience a few months later for me to get more enthusiastic about it.　　　—Fiona, Lawrence, Kansas

Starting Early

I was in third grade hanging out with older kids playing spin the bottle, and an older boy kissed me on my cheek. My heart was racing and it was scary, but I liked the thrill of experimenting and feeling grown up. —Rebecca, Rye, New York

Guys' Perspectives

The Perfect Valentine's Day

I was in first grade when I had my first kiss. It was sometime around Valentine's

Day, and we went through the ritual of giving out Valentine's Day cards to members of our class. I was determined to only give out one Valentine's Day card to the girl that I had a very heavy crush on. She was six years older than I was and her name was Bridget and she was my classmate Chuck's older sister. Chuck was fully aware of my crush, and he would always tease me about it. Because of his big mouth, Bridget also knew about my crush and would always smile at me in a flirtatious way that made me turn my head in embarrassment. She thought I was cute, but in a little brother sort of a way. Every time she smiled at me, I would get bright red and get goose bumps all over. She was the prettiest girl in the school, so she could do this to someone.

I wrote a Valentine's Day poem for her. Later on that day we had a little Valentine's Day party in the classroom, and everyone started to distribute cards and candy. I had a problem because my Valentine wasn't in my class. I consulted with Chuck, and we decided that I would have to give it to the girl in my class whose name was also Bridget, because the note was addressed to BRIDGET. So I slipped it under her chair (that is how we distributed the cards; I guess it was to keep it as anonymous as possible) and returned to my seat, very disappointed because it was the wrong Bridget.

The school day ended, and my friend Chuck asked me to come over to his house after school. When we got there, Chuck ran upstairs and I was sitting in the kitchen, just waiting for him to return. Then it happened. His sister Bridget started to walk toward me. Her approach seemed as if it were in slow motion, each step taking forever to land. When she got to me, she held out her hand and put a wallet-sized picture of herself in my hand. On the back she had written, THANK YOU FOR THE BEAUTIFUL VALENTINE'S DAY CARD. LOVE, BRIDGET. Then she leaned down and gave me a very soft, pleasant, and kind of wet kiss. I was floored. I asked her how she knew, and she explained to me that Chuck had taken the note away from the other Bridget before she even knew it was there, and had given it to her on the bus ride home. I owed him one, that's for sure! I had received what I really wanted most on that Valentine's Day. I had the Valentine that I wanted and the bonus of receiving my first kiss. I would never be the same. (One little footnote: Later that year, before the summer came, the Bridget in my class became my second kiss, but I never told her about the Valentine's Day thing.)   —Eric, Menands, New York

A Friend Indeed!

I was in eighth grade and never had kissed a girl, so my best friend let me borrow his girlfriend so I could try making out. I went over to her house, and we kissed for a while. It was fun, but then after that I ended up kind of liking her, and they were of course still a couple, so it was sort of a bummer.

          —Brian, San Francisco, California

Foreign Kisses

A *Real* French Kiss

I was petrified about kissing because I never had and I was already sixteen. I decided I either wanted it to be with a boyfriend (which I didn't have) or with someone I'd never see again. I was at a beach house with friends and went to teen night at the surf club. I was with two of my friends. We saw two cute guys: One was so good-looking, I knew I didn't have a chance with him, and the other was a surfer dude who seemed more like my type. I came back from getting a Coke, and one of my friends said she needed to talk to me and took me into the bathroom. She said the gorgeous guy (the one I didn't think I had a chance with) wanted to meet me. When we got out of the bathroom, I was all red and flustered; he knew we'd been talking about him. I forced myself to make a little eye contact here and there, and he came over to me. I thought I was gonna die right there, I was frozen in my seat. I didn't even hear what he was saying. We each said hi, but I could barely speak. His name was Jerome, he was seventeen, and he was from Nice, France. He looked like James Van Der Beek. It was really awkward, and the language barrier was huge. So I said, "Let's go for a walk." We went to the beach for a stroll and held hands. I was giddy and laughing; I didn't know what to do. I told him I'd never kissed anyone before, and he said, "Don't worry. You can be the pupil and I'll be the teacher." The next thing I knew, he was kissing me. It was awesome. We kissed for two hours. Then we went back to our friends. It was exactly what I wanted for my first kiss because he taught me, so I stopped worrying about whether I was doing it right.

When the time came for my second kiss, the boy wasn't a good kisser at all, so I ended up teaching him. I was confident because kissing Jerome had been so fabulous that I just knew we had been doing something right. I said, "Let me lead, *I'll* kiss *you*." And that worked.

—Peggy, Bronx, New York

A Prickly British Kiss

My first kiss was with a British exchange student named John, who was just dreamy. I was in tenth grade, and many families in town were hosting British exchange students for a month. The guy staying with my family was icky, but John was just awesome. During that month we hung out all of the time. What I remember most was his big nose and this cool blue and white scarf he used to wear everywhere. The scarf was the team scarf for the Bristol Rovers, his favorite football (soccer) team, and I think he even slept with it because it reminded him of home. So one night one of the kids from school who also was hosting a student had a party. During the party John and I took a walk around the neighborhood to be alone. The whole time I was thinking about what I would do if he tried to kiss me, really kiss me, because I had never done that before. So in my mind I was planning how I would cock my head just the right way so we would match up perfectly. Turns out he was equally nervous. As the walk was nearing its end, he suddenly grabbed me while we started up the driveway. As he was kissing me (we did match up pretty well), we fell backward into the bushes by the side of the driveway, which by then (this was spring) were full of thorns! So it took about ten minutes to get out of that bush because we were stuck on all of the thorns, and they were stuck in us. Of course, he had on that same dumb scarf and he used it to pull the branches off of me. As much as it hurt, I didn't care. I felt so cool going back into that party. My first kiss had been successful, and he and I just laughed the rest of the night about our prickly kiss.   —Belinda, Chicago, Illinois

What Some of the Uninitiated Say About Kissing

"My first kiss will probably be after I'm fourteen. My friends and I are all a little boy-crazy, but I have the rest of my life to kiss. I don't really feel comfortable right now. I have crushes on boys but I just want them to flirt back and like me."

—Lauren, twelve, Park City, Utah

"My first kiss will come when it's time. I do worry that I won't know how to kiss when that time comes, though."

—Channing, thirteen, Hong Kong

"In movies, kissing is okay, but it's just part of the story. I like the romance but I get bored during the really long kisses—I always think, *okay, I get it, they're kissing.*"

—Madeleine, ten, Chicago, Illinois

"The best kisses in movies are short and meaningful, not long or mushy or too intimate. Those are just annoying and weird and boring."

—Zoe, twelve, Los Gatos, California

"When they kiss in the movies it looks a little appealing, but the thought of kissing makes me nervous. My mom says she was so nervous about kissing boys that when she was on dates and it was time to say good-bye, she would run inside and pull the screen door closed so it was between her and her date. She would talk to them and thank them for the evening but make sure to stay behind the screen door. Then she wondered why nobody ever kissed her!"

—Sara, twelve, Park City, Utah

"Most of the only people who kiss are in the popular crowd. They are the ones with big boobs who flirt and laugh or wear tight tops and short shorts."

—Anne, twelve, Atlanta, Georgia

Chapter 5
More Kissing Memories
The Divine and the Disgusting

Even after you've kissed a lot, certain kisses become etched in your memory forever. A kiss can change the way you feel about somebody—for better or for worse.

Dreamiest Kisses

Nervous but Nice

I was in college and taking German and had a big crush on my German tutor. We became friends and hung out together, but he was so beautiful that I was nervous to ask him out. I did, anyway, and he said yes and we went to the theater. I remember thinking the whole time that I couldn't believe I was actually sitting next to him. He drove me home, and we sat in his car outside my mom's building, where I was living, and talked. I was thinking, *should I kiss him?* but I didn't have the nerve.

After a while he said, "I guess I should let you go upstairs," and as I was getting out, he said, "Terry," and I said, "What?" He said, "Aren't you forgetting something?" I checked for my purse, which was on my shoulder, and said, "No." Then he leaned over and said, "I think all dates should end with a kiss." I was completely speechless. Then he gave me the most gentle and tentative kiss I've ever experienced. It was amazing. Then he pulled away a little to see my reaction, and I noticed he was trembling. I said, "Are you okay?" He said, "I am nervous." His gentleness was so sweet and unusual. We kept kissing, softly and slowly. I think the secret of his kissing technique was that he really loved to kiss.

—Terry, Brooklyn, New York

Hot Lips

I had a very tender kissing experience my junior year of high school. I started to date a hottie who was "older and wiser" and not from our high school. One of my good friends set us up. We were in her kitchen alone for the first time and we kissed. I felt my legs tremble and stomach start to warm up like I was sitting in front of a fire. His lips were so soft, and he teased my mouth so gingerly. I think I drooled a bit, and he took his finger and wiped my chin off. He was so sweet and made me realize how incredibly intoxicating kissing can be.

—Johanna, Easton, Pennsylvania

Kissing Disaster Stories

There are all sorts of stories circulating about mortifying kissing misadventures. Two kissers end up with their braces stuck together and need to call on one of their mothers to help unlock them. One kisser with braces bumps the other's lip, gouging the flesh and creating a blood-bath. Gum falls out of one kisser's mouth and into the other's hair—requiring scissors and peanut butter to remove the gum. Somebody burps or hiccups in the middle of a kiss, a parent walks in, or a kiss is unsavory for one reason or another—whether it's nacho breath, too much tongue, or saliva galore. While (thankfully) these smooches gone sour don't happen every day, they aren't completely out of the question. Here are some real-life kissing disaster stories. The good news? The people who shared them lived to tell—and even laugh—about it!

Disaster in Barbados

I was on a trip in Barbados with my family when I was seventeen. The guy lived there, and our families were friends, so he showed me around the island. It was one of my last days before leaving, and we were in his car and he was being really quiet and shy and then he suddenly kissed me. The flying fish is the national fish of Barbados, and that's all I could think of when he leaned down and gave me a wet, icky kiss. I didn't want to hurt his feelings but I was totally repulsed, so I feigned shyness. I had liked him enough to seriously consider kissing him, but that kiss turned me off completely. After that I avoided him till my family left, and then I couldn't even read his letters. It was too bad, because he was cute. I still don't understand what he did to make his kiss so wet.   —Theresa, New City, New York

"He Almost Gave Me a Concussion!"

My boyfriend and I were in Hyde Park in London sitting on a statue kissing. After a little while, I think I must have pulled away for a second to breathe or something. I still wanted to kiss him more, so we were both leaning back into each other to continue our smooching and, for some reason, we didn't tilt our heads, and he knocked me so hard on my forehead that I actually almost fell off the statue. It really hurt. I was rubbing my head for five minutes, saying, "It hurts," and he felt so bad. He said, "Let me look," and he looked at it and then tenderly kissed my forehead where his head had bumped mine. It was so sweet and it got me back in the mood to continue kissing again.

—Theresa, London, England

Caught on the Couch

I had a boyfriend for basically all of high school, and my parents were out a lot, so he'd be over and we'd be kissing on the couch. We'd hear my parents' car and jump up and separate onto different couches. Thinking back, that probably made it look even worse—the fact that we were always so far away from each other when my parents would come home.

But one time we had survived my parents' coming home, and then they went to bed, so we thought we could safely resume our making out. I guess my mom thought she heard the cat scratching to get inside, so she came downstairs and didn't know we were still down there. I didn't even notice her until she'd already been down there for quite a while. But as soon as I looked up from my kissing, I saw my mom looking at us, just kind of standing there surprised. Then she kind of quickly ran upstairs. The whole incident certainly ruined the night, and my boyfriend went home. The next morning I was so afraid to go downstairs. I could only imagine what she had told my father. I stayed upstairs for as long as humanly possible. When I went downstairs, everyone just ignored the whole situation.

—Samantha, West Chester, Pennsylvania

Songs

"The Shoop Shoop Song (It's in His Kiss)," by Cher

"Give Me a Kiss," by Van Morrison

"As Time Goes By" ("You must remember this, a kiss is still a kiss . . ."), by Jimmy Durante, on the *Sleepless in Seattle* CD

"Kiss Me at Midnight," by 'N Sync

"Kissing You," by Des'ree

"Kiss," by Prince

"Kiss Me," by Sixpence None The Richer

"Kissing a Fool," by George Michael

"This Kiss," by Faith Hill

"A Kiss to Build a Dream On," by Louis Armstrong, on the *Sleepless in Seattle* CD

"Vision of a Kiss," by the B-52's

"Shut Up and Kiss Me," by Mary-Chapin Carpenter

"Let's Just Kiss," by Harry Connick, Jr.

"Last Kiss," by Pearl Jam

"Passionate Kisses," by Lucinda Williams

"Prelude to a Kiss," by Duke Ellington

"Pucker Up," by Patty Larkin

"The Kiss," by The Cure

"The Perfect Kiss," by Bette Midler

"Venus Kissed the Moon," by Christine Lavin

"Our First Kiss," by Jonathan Edwards

"I'll Kiss You," by Cyndi Lauper

"Kiss and Tell," by Bryan Ferry

"Kiss from a Rose," by Seal

"Kiss Me in the Rain," by Barbra Streisand

"Kiss on My List" by Hall & Oates

CHAPTER 6

Quotes from Stars on Kissing

Celebrities' First Kisses

Lacey Chabert (*Party of Five*; *Lost in Space*), age fifteen: On her first kiss ever (which happened to be on-screen):

"I had to have my first kiss in front of, like, a hundred people. I didn't know what to do. So my sisters told me to, like, practice on a pillow, you know? But it didn't kiss me back, so I didn't know what to expect. But it was good practice, I guess. It was incredibly embarrassing, but I got through it."

On her first real kiss:

"I had my first boyfriend, actually, when I was filming *Lost in Space* in London. He wasn't in the movie. He was [related] to someone in the movie. . . . [We were] outside of my flat in London. . . . It was the last time I was going to see him. I thought, you know, maybe he would want to kiss me, or whatever. I thought I was going to throw up. And he just looks at me, and says, 'Kiss me.' And we kissed, and it was perfect."

Sharon Stone: "I was in the basement of my parents' house. We were playing darts, and he kissed me. He kissed me, like, KISSED me! Like, wow! Not like your aunt kissing you, but, like, whoa! I was fifteen."

Sandra Bullock: "My cutie-pie neighbor boy kissed me through my bedroom window. He got his little best friend to go on all fours and he stood on his pal's back to get up high enough. Isn't that sweet?"

Brad Pitt (he was in fourth grade): "We actually made a plan at school to meet in her garage and kiss. It was like this little business deal. So I get there. I go right up to her. I kiss her. Then I ran home." (According to a *Teen People* article, Brad Pitt was famous in high school back in Missouri, but not for his acting—he was known for throwing great make-out parties.)

Top Ten Movie Kisses

Watch these movies for awesome, memorable, meaningful kisses:

She's All That: Rachel Leigh Cook and Freddie Prinze, Jr.

Never Been Kissed: Drew Barrymore and Michael Vartan

Ever After: Drew Barrymore and Dougray Scott

Lady and The Tramp: Lady and Tramp (While Lady and Tramp are eating spaghetti, they eat one strand, each starting from an opposite end, and when they meet in the middle, they kiss.)

William Shakespeare's Romeo & Juliet: Claire Danes and Leonardo DiCaprio

Beauty and the Beast: Belle and the Beast

Picture Perfect: Jennifer Aniston and Jay Mohr

Clueless: Alicia Silverstone and Paul Rudd

You've Got Mail: Tom Hanks and Meg Ryan

French Kiss: Kevin Kline and Meg Ryan

Tom Cruise: "There was a time when my older sisters and their friends were just starting to kiss boys. They needed somebody to practice on. I'd sprint home from school, go in the bathroom, they'd put me on the bathroom sink, and my sister's two friends would take turns kissing me. They taught me how to French kiss when I was eight years old. The first time, I almost suffocated."

Supermodel **Mark Vanderloo** about his first date with his new wife, supermodel Esther Cañadas: "We kissed, and it was the longest kiss I ever had. From that moment, it was a done deal."

Martha Plimpton (*Beautiful Girls; My Life's in Turnaround*): "I know it sounds weird, but I couldn't kiss someone knowing their saliva had impurities."

Stars on On-screen Kisses

Emily Bergl (*The Rage: Carrie 2*):
"I was rehearsing the balcony scene from *Romeo and Juliet* with Neil Patrick Harris. He was supposed to jump up and

steal a kiss from me—only I got a little overzealous. I knocked teeth with him, and he fell off the balcony! Not exactly the romantic moment the director was looking for."

Kate Winslet (*Titanic*; *Sense and Sensibility*; *Hideous Kinky*): On kissing Leonardo DiCaprio: "He was just a joy to work with. . . . But right before we had to do our first kissing scene . . . we were both, like, 'Oh, here we go,' and were silly and having a laugh about it. Then we kissed, and each of us went, 'Aaah, yuck.' It was like kissing my brother, and he said it was like kissing his sister."

Michael Vartan (Drew Barrymore's English teacher in *Never Been Kissed*; also in *The Pallbearer*; *The Myth of Fingerprints*): "Oh my god! It was honestly one of the best kisses I've ever had—and it was a movie kiss. I can't even imagine how good it would have been if we were in a room alone. I'd say we kissed for a good three hours. On and off, of course. It wasn't enough."

Kissable Cuties

The Swedish have a word for "kissable": *kysst*. But you don't need to know Swedish to recognize what all these guys have in common:

Seth Green (*Can't Hardly Wait;* *Idle Hands;* and both Austin Powers movies)

Will Smith (*Men in Black; Wild, Wild West; Independence Day*)

Brian and Kevin (Backstreet Boys)

David Schwimmer (*Friends*)

Matt Damon (*The Talented Mr. Ripley, All the Pretty Horses*)

Carson Daly (MTV VJ)

Eric, Shawn, Corey, and Jack (*Boy Meets World*)

Ricky Martin ("Livin' la Vida Loca")

Ben Affleck (*Dogma, Reindeer Games, Boiler Room*)

Freddie Prinze, Jr. (*Down to You, Head over Heels*)

Brad Pitt (*Meet Joe Black; Legends of the Fall; Seven Years in Tibet; Seven*)

Tyrese (video jockey and singer)

Chapter 7
The Science of Kissing

It's no wonder kissing is such a big deal. Our bodies are actually programmed to enjoy it. Kissing signals our brains to produce oxytocin, a hormone that gives us an all-over great sensation, one that feels almost like we're melting.

Also, inside our mouths and at the edges of our lips are sebaceous skin glands that produce a substance called sebum, which is thought to make us want to keep kissing once we've begun. That explains why it's so hard to stop kissing and also why we sometimes get that addicted feeling when we really like someone. Our lips are also hundreds of times more sensitive than our fingertips, which explains why holding hands is fun, but kissing is better! And our brains have special neurons that help us locate each other's lips in the dark. This comes in pretty handy when you're dancing to a slow dance and the lights are dim.

Kissing in the Wild

Birds Do It, Snails Do It, Porcupines Do It!

* Snails rub antennae together.
* Birds caress beaks.
* Dogs lick masters and kiss each other when they are playing.
* The kissing gourami is a pink or green-white tropical fish that kisses other gouramis on the mouth for up to twenty-five minutes.
* North American porcupines nuzzle the tips of each other's noses—one of the few places on their bodies without quills.
* Chimpanzees kiss more like humans than any other animal.

Why Kissing is Good for Us

* Kissing exfoliates rough spots on your lips, keeping them nice and soft for future kisses.
* A ten-minute kiss burns ten calories.
* Studies have shown that people who kiss their spouses every morning are healthier than those who don't. They also have fewer car accidents on the way to work, earn more money, and live an average of five years longer. Some believe that's because they begin each day with a positive attitude.
* Kissing reduces blood pressure and tension.
* Kissing is also good for your teeth because it increases saliva flow, which washes food particles away, which prevents plaque buildup and promotes healthy teeth.

The Gross News About Kissing

* An old Burt Bacharach and Hal David song complains that kissing will give you "enough germs to catch pneumonia." Kissing isn't exactly a germ-free pastime.

* There are 278 colonies of bacteria that are passed in kissing. Thankfully 95 percent of them are harmless.
* Mono (short for mononucleosis) is often called the kissing disease. It's a viral infection that leaves you weak, tired, and with a sore throat and swollen glands for weeks or even months. It is known as the kissing disease, but there are other ways to get it—like sharing utensils or being coughed on by someone with it. So, if you get the kissing disease, rest assured that you won't be kissing anybody again for a while. . . .
* But don't be scared off. Kissing is, in general, safe unless one of the kissers is sick.

Kissing in Other Countries

* In some African cultures, mothers kiss children, but adults don't share romantic kisses.
* The Chinese used to feel a kiss was indecent even in private. Now for the most part they still do not kiss in public.

* When the French greet each other, they kiss twice—once on each cheek.
* In Belgium and certain regions of France and Switzerland, people kiss three times on the cheek.
* Austrians are famous for kissing on the hand.
* Laplanders kiss on the mouth and rub noses at the same time.
* The Japanese did not kiss before they were exposed to the West.
* Indonesians kiss only on the cheek.
* Germans have thirty words for kissing. They even have one, *Nachkus,* for a kiss given to make up for ones that were overlooked in the past.
* Greeks kiss each other hello on the lips.
* Finlanders consider mouth-to-mouth kissing obscene.
* Eskimos, Malaysians, Polynesians, and Balinese kiss mostly by rubbing noses.
* A ban against mouth kissing in the movies was recently lifted in India.

Advanced Kissing Games for Couples

* When you're watching TV or a video-tape with a cutie pie, you can kiss each other whenever the actors do.

* A variation of the above game is to kiss each other whenever there's a commercial break.

* Morse code kiss: Find a Morse code chart and, using long and short kisses, spell out messages for each other to decipher.

* Alphabet kiss: Try making the letters of the alphabet with your tongue while you're kissing. Take turns guessing what letter you are each drawing.

* Pick a "magic" word and, every time either of you says it, you have to kiss each other.

* Life Saver game: Put a Life Saver (or any candy with a hole in the center) on a string, then each of you put an end of the string in your mouth. Race to get to the Life Saver, and the winner gets a kiss from the loser.

* Share a packet of Pop Rocks and then kiss, adding extra fireworks to your smooching session.

* Next time you go to an amusement park, try to kiss your sweetie while on a roller coaster, right at the top, before you go down. See how long you can hold it before you scream or laugh.

* Follow the leader: Agree to kiss for a whole minute how you like to be kissed; then switch so you kiss for an entire minute the way he likes to be kissed. You'll discover that learning has never been so much fun!

Chapter 8
Kissing Trivia

* The longest kiss that ever took place was in Chicago in 1984. It lasted seventeen days and ten and one-half hours.
* One man, Alfred E. Wofram, kissed 10,504 people in eight hours on August 19, 1990, in New Brighton, Minnesota.
* Before she gets married, the average woman will kiss seventy-nine men.
* The longest underwater kiss was in Tokyo, Japan, on April 2, 1980. It lasted two minutes, eighteen seconds.
* During a six-mile pilgramage to Lhasa, a devout Buddhist will kiss the ground over thirty thousand times.
* A recent internet survey found that 58 percent of people asked would rather kiss than star in the latest Batman movie.
* From that same survey, 47 percent said they like to spend at least four hours a day kissing.

* In that same survey, 5 percent said they wish they'd never heard of kissing.
* 81 percent prefer to kiss with their eyes closed.
* The first kiss ever to be shown in a movie was in 1896. The name of the movie? *The Kiss.*
* 86 percent of Americans say they experienced a first romantic kiss in their early- or mid-teens. A recent *YM* poll found the average age of its readers when they first kissed was twelve years old.
* Most kisses in the United States last no longer than a minute.
* A *YM* poll of its readers found that many dream of stars at night: 32 percent had dreamed of Matt Damon; 30 percent of Ben Affleck; 14 percent of James Van Der Beek; 10 percent of Will Smith; 8 percent of Brad Pitt; and 4 percent of Leonardo DiCaprio; 56 percent of the dreams involved kissing.

Great Art Inspired by a Kiss

All these works are called *The Kiss*:

Auguste Rodin: marble sculpture, 1886

Henri de Toulouse-Lautrec: oil painting, 1892

Edvard Munch: oil painting, 1892

Gustav Klimt: oil painting, 1907

Constantin Brancusi: stone sculpture, 1907

Pablo Picasso: oil painting, 1904

Roy Lichtenstein: *The Kiss*, pop art, 1962

Adolphe-William Bouguereau: *The First Kiss*, oil painting, 1873

Chapter 9
Quiz: Are You Ready to Kiss?

1. You think boys

a. are adorable; you think about them all the time.
b. are mostly immature, but *your* boyfriend (or the guy you *wish* was your boyfriend) is the best.
c. are fun to play kickball with but you can't imagine being alone with one, let alone kissing one!
d. are dumb and have cooties.

2. Complete this sentence: It would be great if

a. I could kiss every boy I have a crush on.
b. the boy I like would like me back and we could go to movies together and talk on the phone, dance together at dances, and maybe hold hands.
c. I could hang out with a boy without having to worry about kissing him.

d. everybody would just stop talking about kissing.

3. Kissing in general

a. is the most awesome thing; you can't wait to kiss your next victim!
b. looks like a lot of fun, but you still can't imagine doing it anytime soon.
c. is just a way to become popular or to get a boy to like you.
d. looks gross and like a way to spread germs.

4. Your first kiss

a. will be with a special someone in a really romantic setting, just like it happens in the movies.
b. better happen soon; you're so sick of being the only one who hasn't smooched.
c. is something that, every time you think about it, makes you laugh. All those boys in your class are so stupid, why would you ever kiss them?
d. is something you haven't even thought of yet.

5. At school dances, you

a. ask boys to dance; talk and laugh with them. Sometimes, if one looks you in the eyes, your heart pounds and you blush—in other words, you're thrilled.
b. dance with boys but don't look at them in the eyes—instead, you talk to your friends.
c. treat all the boys like brothers and joke around with them without ever getting too close.
d. sit or stand in a corner with your friends, don't ask any boys to dance, and are happy nobody asks you to dance.

6. When you watch a movie and there's hot and heavy kissing, you think

a. that looks like they are really meant to be together. I hope that happens to me soon, maybe with that cute guy in seventh grade.
b. how in the world will that ever happen to me?
c. I doubt people really kiss like that.
d. yawn. When is this boring part going to end?

7. You are at a party and people start talking about playing spin the bottle. You

a. drag your best friend into the bathroom with you so she can check your breath.
b. feel like you're going to puke, but stay right there so you don't miss any of the action.
c. decide that you don't want your first kiss to be a public display of affection, and announce that you're not going to play.
d. sneak to a phone and call your mom to beg her to come to pick you up.

8. Your best friend tells you that the best friend of Scott (a real hottie) told you Scott has a crush on you. He's a sweetie, too, but he's already had a girlfriend, and you know that they've French kissed. You

a. figure that he'll be happy to show you the ropes, and you start talking to him, flirting, so he knows you're willing.
b. figure he won't like you once he finds out you've never kissed a boy, so you avoid him and ignore him.
c. are flattered that he likes you, but now

that you know he might want to French kiss you, you can't help but be a little grossed out when you see him.

d. aren't interested, period!

9. You want to kiss boys because

a. you have a boyfriend or are majorly crushing on this one guy, and you want to be close to him.
b. you want to get your first kiss over with because all your friends already have and you're really curious about what it will be like.
c. if it weren't for the fact that the kids in the popular crowd are all kissing, you'd never even think about kissing.
d. you don't want to kiss boys.

10. Complete this sentence: I would rather _____ than kiss.

a. there's nothing I'd rather do than kiss the boy I like.
b. hold hands, flirt, and hang out with a guy
c. get to have my best friend sleep over every night for a week
d. do anything, even take a pop quiz or drink clam juice

Why Kiss?

Here is what some of you said
when asked why people kiss:

"It's a sign of affection."

"It makes you feel special and wanted."

"Because they are dared to."

"Because they like someone and can't control themselves."

"So you can go back to school and tell your friends."

"Because they are perverts."

"Because they love each other."

"Because they want to brag and be popular."

"I've never done it, but I think it's overrated."

"Because they just want to."

Give yourself four points for every time you answered a; three points for every b; two points for every c; and one point for every d answer. What it means:

If you got between thirty-one and forty points, you may be ready for a kiss. Maybe you have a boyfriend, but even if you don't, you're definitely boy-crazy. You are a romantic and a flirt and you have a sense of adventure about kissing. Just make sure it's for the right reasons—and that you're not doing it to please someone else, whether it's a boy you like or the cool crowd. If you kiss before you're ready, you might end up not liking it as much as you will if you wait.

If you got between twenty-one and thirty points, you long for romance but are more interested in feeling wanted and having someone to flirt with than to swap spit (for now). You may be feeling a little peer pressure to kiss, but just enjoy the fun of the chase for the time being. The waiting and anticipation can make the kissing even more wonderful.

If you got between eleven and twenty points, you are conflicted about your feelings about boys. You're comfortable around them as friends but haven't spent much time thinking about them romantically. You may feel a little peer pressure because others are kissing, but it doesn't really appeal to you yet. You'd best hold off until you're really ready (you'll know) or you may be majorly disappointed.

If you got fewer than eleven points, you have a while before you will be ready to kiss, but it seems like you are mature and smart enough to know that. After all, you have your whole life to kiss—why start now when you still feel like being a kid?

Chapter 10
What's His Sign?

Each astrological sign is believed to have tendencies to view the world or behave in a certain way. Below is a sneak peek into what kind of kisses a boy might give, depending on his sign. So find out his birthday if you don't already know it, and read up on ways to win his heart—and his lips.

♂ ARIES (March 21–April 19): If your Aries crush wants to kiss you, he probably will. Aries are go-getters. But they also would probably not mind one bit if you made the first move. Aries like boldness—and they love kissing. Tip: Playing hard to get (just a little) might make you even more appealing to him. Best matches: Leo, Sagittarius, and Libra. Famous Aries hotties: Ewan McGregor (March 31); Austin Peck (April 9).

✳ TAURUS (April 20–May 20): Taurus might be slow to make the first move,

70

but be patient—because it will be worth the wait. Your crush will be more likely to kiss you if you are friends first. The problem is that Taurus, a creature of habit, might not necessarily be able to make the transition without some help from you. Taurus can get jealous, so give him some chocolate (his favorite) and reassure him that he is your *numero uno*. Best matches: Virgo, Capricorn, Scorpio. Famous Taurus hotties: Lance Bass (May 4); Kenan Thompson (May 10).

GEMINI (May 21–June 21): Geminis are known for being big flirts. They are also fickle and indecisive, so if your crush is a Gemini, he might have a hard time making up his mind about whether to kiss or not to kiss. But luckily you can help him decide by charming him with sparkling conversation. Tip: Finding new and different ways to kiss him will keep him coming back for more. Gemini craves constant variety. Best matches: Libra, Sagittarius, Aquarius. Famous hottie Geminis: Josh Jackson (June 11); Noah Wyle (June 4).

CANCER (June 22–July 22): If your

cutie pie is a Cancer, you're in for a treat, because Cancers give amazing hugs. They're not afraid of romance (or kissing) and they also know that nice presents, sensitivity, and humor are almost as romantic as a smooch. Tip: Bring him his favorite food and he will be yours. Best matches: Pisces, Scorpio, Capricorn. Famous Cancer hotties: Carson Daly (June 22); Prince William (June 21).

LEO (July 23–August 23): Your Leo is a real romantic! He also probably lives for flattery, and loves to laugh. If you are affectionate and attentive, you can expect his kisses to be enthusiastic. He likes to play teacher, so if you're a kissing novice, you're in the right hands. Best matches: Aries, Sagittarius, Aquarius. Famous Leo hotties: Ben Affleck (August 15); Matt LeBlanc (July 25).

VIRGO (August 23–September 22): Your Virgo cutie pie is loyal and dependable, probably the one friends call when they need to talk. He is probably a conscientious student, so if you invite him over to do homework, he may actually want to do homework.

Virgos also have a reputation for being perfectionists—some would say neat freaks. So clean your room and brush your teeth twice, just in case. Good news: Virgos are amazing kissers. Best matches: Capricorn, Taurus, Pisces. Famous Virgo hotties: Adam Sandler (September 9); Ryan Phillippe (September 10).

♎ LIBRA (September 23–October 23): If you're crushing on a Libra, don't expect your first kiss to be in public. It might be hard to tell at first where you stand with your Libra lad because he probably flirts with everyone, not just you. You'll probably spend a lot of time talking before the big moment, since he thrives on interesting conversation. Hint: Libras are suckers for sappy gifts. Best matches: Aquarius, Gemini, Aries. Famous Libra hotties: Will Smith (September 25); Matt Damon (October 8).

♏ SCORPIO (October 24–November 21): You might be wondering whether your Scorpio crush likes you or not. Scorpios tend to be mysterious and secretive, so it's not easy to tell whether they're thinking of kissing you or dissing you. Remember this: Scorpios are also known as the most passionate sign, so chances are good he is keen on kissing. When they like someone, Scorpios think kissing is total heaven (and you will, too). But be careful, because Scorpios get very jealous. Best matches: Taurus, Pisces, Cancer. Famous hottie Scorpios: Leonardo DiCaprio (November 11); Matthew McConaughey (November 4).

SAGITTARIUS (November 22–December 21): Sagittarius likes an adventure, so get your Sag outdoors if you want a kiss. Another idea: If you are old enough to drive, try stealing a kiss in the car or while in-line skating: Sagittarius likes to be on the move. If you find yourself getting jealous because he's talking to another girl, don't be surprised. Sagittarius boys are known flirts. Best matches: Aries, Leo, Gemini. Famous Sagittarius hotties: Brendan Fraser (December 3); Jakob Dylan (December 9).

CAPRICORN (December 22–January 19): If you like a Capricorn, the best way to get a kiss is to kiss him first. Or at least start the ball rolling by inviting him somewhere. Capricorns are famous for controlling their emotions, so you may need to help loosen him up. Though Capricorns are hard workers, they also have a very silly side, so smooching one can be fun-filled. Best matches: Taurus, Virgo, Cancer. Famous Capricorn hotties: Skeet Ulrich (January 20); Tiger Woods (December 30).

AQUARIUS (January 20–February 18): Aquarius has a rep for being offbeat and daring. You will impress him when you show that you have a wild side, too. Don't woo him with the tra-ditional heart-shaped Valentine's Day card. Instead, surprise him with a cre-ative e-mail. Try not to rush Aquarius into romance, because being friends first is important to him. Hint: Once you've won his heart, try out some innovative kisses on him. Best matches: Leo, Gemini, Libra. Famous Aquarius hotties: Elijah Wood (January 28); Andrew Keegan (January 29).

PISCES (February 19-March 20): Pisces is very imaginative and is ruled by emotions. He can also be very shy. To get your Pisces in the mood, hold his hand, listen to what he's saying, and try to relate to how he's feeling. You will know if he likes you because he will pay a lot of attention to you. Do you live near the ocean, a lake, or even a pond? Your best bet is to try to steal a kiss by a body of water. Best matches: Cancer, Scorpio, Virgo. Famous Pisces hotties: James Van Der Beek (March 8); Antonio Sabàto, Jr. (February 29).

Kissing Customs

Mistletoe—A Christmas custom: If you are standing underneath a piece of this green shrub, a popular Christmas decoration, you get to kiss whomever's standing there with you.

Blowing a kiss—In Mesopotamia in 3000 B.C., worshipers threw kisses to their gods.

The Blarney stone—It's built into the wall of Blarney Castle, near Cork, Ireland. It is supposed to give anyone who kisses it the skill to speak, through flattery, his or her way out of any danger. (It is said that the castle's protectors once saved it from destruction this way.)

Kissing Frogs—In the Grimm fairy tale "The Frog Prince," a witch puts a spell on a handsome prince that turns him into a frog. The only thing that can save him is the kiss of a girl (which the witch assumes will never happen, because who would kiss a slimy frog?). The moral of the story: Even something that looks repulsive may be quite lovable.

Any woman who kisses the statue of sixteenth-century Italian soldier Guidarello Guidarelli is supposed to marry and settle down with a great man. Over 5 million women have kissed it, but the number of those who ended up marrying great men remains unreported.

Top Ten TV Shows to Watch for Great Kisses

Boy Meets World
Dharma and Greg
Two Guys and a Girl
Brotherly Love
Buffy the Vampire Slayer
Jesse
Spin City
Friends
Seventh Heaven
Promised Land

Chapter 11
Q&A

Here are some common questions about kissing, along with answers to give you basic guidelines. But remember to try not to overthink the how-to part. If you have a general idea, and you keep practicing, the rest will come naturally. Guaranteed.

* * * * * * * *

Q. I don't get what you're supposed to do with your lips when you're kissing a boy. In movie kisses, actors' lips look totally different from the pucker I'm used to making when kissing relatives.

A. You can still gently pucker—but try to keep your lips much more relaxed and loose than they are when you're kissing your mom or great-aunt. The insides of our lips, the part not usually exposed to the air, is the softest part and therefore the nicest part to kiss. Think of the way you hold your mouth when you're drinking from a water fountain, not open but not entirely closed—and definitely not tense. If you start kissing for longer periods, you can vary the pressure of your lips.

Q. When do I breathe and swallow during a long kiss?

A. It's important not to forget to breathe, because you can make yourself dizzy, and also you might end up producing too much saliva, which makes for a sloppy kiss. Another bonus about breathing: You can kiss for longer, without having to break for air. So how do you breathe? Lightly through your nose. Note: If your kissing partner is gasping, that could mean he is having trouble breathing, possibly because you are squashing his nose. As far as swallowing, you can swallow your own saliva while kissing—or take little tiny breaks to swallow.

Q. What do you do with your tongue during a French kiss? Are both of our tongues supposed to be moving around at the same time?

A. Yes, think of it like your tongues are slow dancing—slow, smooth, and varied rhythms.

Q. How long does a kiss last?
A. As long as you want it to. Sometimes the best kisses are short and sweet; others are marathons.

Q. How do I end a kiss?
A. First of all, remember you can stop anytime you want. Maybe you're getting a crick in your neck or you're feeling out of breath, or maybe you just feel like it's getting too intense and making you uncomfortable. The ideal way is to gently pull your head back and close your mouth. You can also end with an encore: a quick dry kiss on the lips or cheek.

Q. What do you say or do afterward?
A. Smiling is always nice. Don't worry too much about what to say; you're both in the same boat.

Q. Are my eyes supposed to be open or closed?
A. Most people close their eyes while they kiss, probably because that's the way it's done in the movies. Closing your eyes can help you focus on, and enjoy, the

moment. Note: Be careful not to close your eyes too soon or you could bump noses as you're moving in for the kiss!

Some people like to look while they're kissing, or at least sneak quick peeks—which is a compliment to the person they are kissing. This does not mean that if the person closes his eyes it is an insult—keeping your eyes open can be uncomfortable because it's so intimate.

Q. I wear glasses and I keep thinking of that saying "Boys don't make passes at girls who wear glasses." Is there any truth to that?

A. Not at all. First of all, glasses can be a totally cool accessory. Second of all, why wait for a boy to make a pass? But if you are too shy to make the first move, don't worry that no boy will ever try to kiss you. Glasses are not likely to get in the way while kissing, especially if only one person wears them. Even if both of you wear glasses, a quick peck is still doable. But if you want to be safe, you could take off your glasses—or take off the glasses of the person you're about to kiss. Note: If you both choose to keep your glasses on and they do bump and click, you'll probably laugh, which can be a good tension breaker. Then you can both take them off and kiss again.

Q. Should I tell my mom when I kiss a boy?

A. It depends on both your relationship with your mom and how you think she will react. If your mom encourages you to be open, and she talks freely about things that are sort of embarrassing, then she would probably like for you to share this exciting event with her, and it might be nice for you to be able to talk to her about it. On the other hand, if your parents might flip out, you probably know it, and you'd best keep your smooch to yourself. (After all, you don't want to end up like Samantha on *The Simpsons*, whose parents sent her away to St. Sebastian's School for Wicked Girls after they found out that she had been kissing Milhouse.) Hopefully your parents aren't that strict, but be a little understanding because it is difficult for many parents to accept that their children are growing up.

Q. My friend and I have spent hours trying to figure out how on earth people kiss without bumping noses. Where do you put your nose? What if you both go to the same side? How does that work?

A. Each person tilts his or her head slightly, and then both noses have a place to go. Sometimes your partner will tilt to his left, and you will tilt to your right, and you will have a collision. It's not the worst thing in the world, but it can be a little embarrassing. It's best to either ignore it or even better to laugh. Kissing is a fun, festive activity, and laughter usually makes it even more fun.

Q. I don't like the way my boyfriend kisses, but I really like him. What should I do? I don't want to hurt his feelings.

A. If you want to change how someone kisses, you need to communicate. You can try some gentle coaching, like: "Let's try kissing with a little less tongue." It seems really hard, but telling him what you like is better for both of you than continuing to kiss him when you aren't enjoying it. Or, sometime, preferably when you're not already in the middle of kissing, you could say you want to experiment the next time you kiss, by taking the lead for a while. Or when you're watching TV or a movie and a kiss looks good to you, lean over to him and whisper that you'd like to try to kiss like that.

Try not to be too critical, because people can be very sensitive about their kissing technique. You definitely don't want him to feel like a loser who can't kiss, or he may avoid you. If you let him know you really like him and are just trying to make a good thing better, he will be more open to your suggestions. Keep in mind that many new couples don't get it perfect from the get-go. It usually takes some getting used to.

If you've talked about it and you still don't like kissing him, it could be he isn't the guy for you. Maybe you don't have any chemistry and you're better off as friends. Another possibility: Sometimes it's a matter of bad timing—are you worried your dad is going to peek out the window and see you two at the front door? Did you just chow down on a bag of Doritos? Do you have a ton of math homework to do? Try to prepare ahead of time (see Chapter 12) and set a more romantic tone.

Q. I like this boy who is a lot taller than I am. I think he likes me, too, but I worry that he'll never ask me out or try to kiss me because of our height difference. Is it hopeless?
A. A lot of couples have a big height difference, and it is definitely a surmountable obstacle. You can stand on something, like a curb, when you think the mood is right, to make a kiss from you more within his reach. Other tips: The taller person can lean against something like a car or a piece of furniture, or you both can sit.

Q. What am I supposed to do with my arms?
A. People often put their arms around the other person's waist or shoulders, like they're hugging. (Then, if you've been in a marathon kissing session, you can start to play with his hair a little or rub the back of his neck gently, like they do in the movies.)

Q. I chew gum to make sure my breath is

fresh, but should I spit it out before I start kissing?

A. Gum is generally a bad idea while kissing, because it's just one more thing in your mouth that you have to think about. You can discreetly spit it out when you sense a kiss is coming in the near future. Of course you could keep the gum in and make it part of the fun by exchanging gum mid-kiss, but some people might think that is gross.

Q. Should I wear lipstick or lip gloss when I kiss?

A. Don't worry if you already have some on, but it's not a great idea to put it on right before a kiss. If it's a noticeable color, it can get all over the boy, and everyone will know you've been kissing. Also, lip gloss or lipstick sometimes has a funny taste that guys don't like. A recent kissing survey found that 85 percent of men prefer to kiss unlipsticked lips.

Q. In the movies it looks so choreographed the way they move their heads back and forth while they kiss. What are they doing, and how do they know how?

A. Both people often rock their heads slowly from one side to the other during longer kissing sessions. It comes naturally and doesn't involve any choreography, so don't worry too much about it. But if you're feeling tense and like a robot while you're kissing, visualize a movie kiss and it might help you (and your partner) relax and get more into it.

Q. Sometimes when I am kissing, it gets really wet. Am I the one to blame or is it that guys are sloppy kissers?
A. To figure out whether it's you or he, pull back a little and swallow before you continue kissing. If the wetness stops now that you've swallowed, then you were probably the one to blame for the drooling. (If it's him, see question on page 84 about what to do if you don't like the way somebody kisses.) The best way to avoid being a sloppy kisser is to remember to keep swallowing.

Q. Will our teeth touch, or is it just mostly tongue and lips?
A. Teeth don't usually get involved during a kiss, but they can bump if either or

both of you are pressing too forcefully. It can be slightly embarrassing, but it's nothing to worry about. You can try to go back to simple non-French kisses for a while if it keeps happening.

Q. I have to get braces next month. Will they stop boys from wanting to kiss me? If I kiss a guy will he be able to feel my braces? (Will they hurt him?) If I kiss a guy who also has braces, are we going to end up stuck together?
A. If somebody likes you, your braces aren't going to stop him from wanting to kiss you. People don't need to worry as much as they do about the perils of kissing with braces. If you have braces and he doesn't, try to keep your kisses gentle, because the only way you'd cut your partner's lips with your braces is if you're kissing forcefully. It is *possible* for hooks and wires to get stuck if both kissers have braces, but it's very unlikely—and you can always get unstuck.

Q. I'm too nervous to kiss my boyfriend. I really want to, but as soon as we get close, I panic.

A. Try to depressurize the moment. Remind yourself he's probably nervous, too, and that no kiss is going to make or break the romance. It's an adventure, so take it slowly and keep the first one short and sweet. If you like each other, you will have time to develop a smooch that fits you both.

You can also slowly work your way up to a kiss together. Ask him to start by kissing your hand; then the next time he can kiss your wrist; and the next time, your arm; then your cheek. By the time he gets to a quick peck on your mouth, you'll probably be a little calmer about the whole idea of him kissing you.

Q. When my boyfriend and I kiss, we sometimes make these smacking noises, and it's kind of embarrassing. Are we doing something wrong? Is there anything we can do about it?

A. You're not doing anything wrong. Why do you think the word "smack" is used for "kiss"? Ignore it or laugh about it. Better yet, put on some music before your next make-out session (see section in Chapter 12 on music to kiss to).

Q. Will he know I've never kissed?
A. Probably not if you don't tell him. But relationships built on honesty are the best, so you might be smart to tell him. Also, it might be fun for you both if he plays kissing teacher and you play his student.

Chapter 12
Getting in the Mood

Places to Kiss

✳ Parties can be good places for kisses. You have the comfort of knowing your friends are nearby, and everyone is usually in a good mood. Public displays of affection (otherwise known as P.D.A.) are not very cool (they can make people jealous and are just sort of tacky), so find a private spot, like around a corner or in the backyard. That doesn't mean people won't notice that you and Mark are off somewhere together, so if you're embarrassed by the thought of others knowing that you are kissing, a party might not be a good spot for you to pucker up.

✳ Dances are also conducive to kissing because there is a hint of romance in the air, with music playing, couples dancing closely, and dim lighting.

✳ Outside in general is also nice. Taking a walk can be a perfect prelude to a smooching session.

✳ Movies have always been thought of as a great place to kiss. It's dark, there's music, often a romantic plot, and you feel alone but there are actually people all around you, so you also feel safe. On the other hand, it can be a bit awkward—if you're not expecting a kiss and you're concentrating on the movie, someone trying to kiss you could alarm you. Plus, maybe one of you really wants to watch the movie and the other one has kissing on his or her mind. You are also facing the same direction, so it's logistically difficult for it to "just happen." There's also, of course, the kissing-in-public factor to consider. Some people don't mind at all, while others would rather be seen in public with their parents than be seen kissing!

When *YM* asked its readers some of the spots where they've kissed, here were the results:

their house (82 percent)
outside (79 percent)
at a party (78 percent)
in a car (76 percent)
at the movies (67 percent)
at school (66 percent)
while baby-sitting (19 percent)

Preparing for a Kiss

It's normal that you're going to worry about your breath. After all, when has anyone ever gotten so close to you before? Try not to let fears about your breath paralyze you. There are, of course, measures you can take to make sure you don't have dragon breath. Here are some ways to make you more kissable:

* Brush your teeth right before you leave the house.
* Leave your retainer at home so you don't have to worry about where to put it and if you're going to lose it.
* Keep your lips soft and moist with Chap Stick or lip gloss.

* Don't apply fresh lipstick if it seems that a kiss is in the air.
* Chew gum or suck on a mint.
* Or if you want to mask the fact that you were freshening your breath in anticipation of a kiss, you can suck on a piece of candy like a Jolly Rancher, so you have sweet delicious breath instead. And then he won't know you were thinking of nothing else but kissing him.

Music to Kiss To

Aerosmith: "I Don't Want to Miss a Thing"
Savage Garden: "Truly Madly Deeply"
'N Sync: "God Must Have Spent a Little More Time on You"
Ricky Martin: "Private Emotion"
The entire sound track to *You've Got Mail*
B*witched: "Blame it on the Weatherman"
98 Degrees: "True to Your Heart"
anything by TLC, Britney Spears, Jennifer Lopez

Practice

* One Colorado girl says she and her friends take turns kissing the bottom of a glass while the others critique the kiss and give pointers.
* Watch how people kiss in movies and on television (see pages 48 and 78).
* Some people like to practice on the back of their hand, so they know what their lips feel like.
* Some like to practice on a pillow. The only problem is that it doesn't kiss back, and your mouth can get dry if you practice for a long time.
* Others practice on a mirror. That way they can get comfortable with the idea of being so close to someone. (Though of course being close to your own reflection is nothing like being close to a cute boy!)
* Kiss a picture in a magazine. A fun variation: Instead of pin the tail on the donkey, this game is called kiss the lips of the boy. (What you need: a poster of a hottie—like Brian from Backstreet Boys—dark lipstick; a blindfold; friends.) Put dark lipstick

on. When it's your turn, the others blindfold you and spin you around and then let you loose to try to kiss Brian's lips. The person whose lip marks are the closest to Brian's luscious lips wins.

* Use your imagination. Think about someone you would like to kiss, close your eyes, and imagine him sitting there and what his lips look like, and think about kissing him. If you've already kissed Seth Green, just think how much easier it will be to smooch the boy from down the street!

Chapter 13
French Kissing

French kissing is definitely a step beyond the regular kiss. It can feel wet and slimy, especially at first. When you're French kissing someone, in some ways it's like you are each opening up and exchanging what's inside of you. It's not ideal for a first kiss—it's best after you're very comfortable with the person, since it can be so intimate.

If You Want to Initiate a French Kiss

It's best to go into French kissing as an extension of the standard kiss. So start by kissing with your mouth closed and then gently open your mouth, just a little. Your heart might start racing, and it might feel weird and awesome all at once. Your partner will probably follow your lead and open his mouth ever so slightly as well. If he doesn't, maybe he doesn't want to French kiss—or maybe he doesn't know what to do.

This is when you can start to test the waters and use your tongue. Start with just the tip. Meet him halfway, and when your tongues meet, you will most certainly be surprised by the way it feels. When you first feel his tongue, you may want to giggle, or you may feel slightly queasy, or you may freeze up. Try to relax and just think of it as a slow dance with your tongues. But you will probably get used to it and even learn to really enjoy it. You can also take your tongue away and see what he does. If he starts it up again, you know you are on the same wavelength. Other tips: Varying the pressure and rhythm makes for a nice kiss. Start soft and gentle and then you can press harder with both your tongue and lips now and then.

If you don't like French kissing, there's nothing wrong with you; some people just don't like it. And most people who do like it now say that it took some getting used to. It could also be that the particular guy you're kissing isn't right for you. Here are some people's initial reactions to French kissing.

A French Kiss at the Movies

My first French kiss was horrible. I wasn't expecting it, and I didn't know what it was when it happened. I was in tenth grade, and my boyfriend and I were in the movie theater seeing *Beauty and the Beast*. After it was over and the closing credits music was playing, I knew it was coming—he was closing in on me, and I didn't know what to do. It was all of five seconds, but it seemed like an eternity. It was all warm and soft and gross. I didn't want to ever do it again. . . . But I jumped back on the horse and kissed him on our next date, and it got better. Since then I've had kisses that have completely turned around the way I feel about a guy.

—Jen, Weston, Connecticut

Yuk and Yay

My first French kiss was after a high school dance. I was standing outside by the entrance of the gym, talking to this guy, Mike, who was a hottie. It suddenly became clear that he was about to kiss me, and I was excited. I had been kissed before, so I detected that look in his eye, but my previous kisses had all been tongue-free. The next thing, there was a beast in my mouth. The look of surprise on my face probably included my jaw dropping, so he took it as a welcoming gesture and kept going. I thought it was pretty disgusting, but it was sort of like with horror movies, where I was thinking *yuk* and *yay* at the same time.

—Sue, Lexington, Massachusetts

The Tongue That Wouldn't Stop

I was in seventh grade when I had my first hookup, at a party in my friend's basement. It was a small party, and everyone was breaking off into couples. I was among the last and I figured I'd better go so I didn't end up alone. This guy, Mark, lured me into the bathroom. Everyone else had staked out dark corners, and even the laundry room was taken. I was excited and nervous. My best friend, Missy, and I had speculated about kissing but had never gotten close. Mark started kissing me on the lips, then on my cheek, then on my ear—then from ear to ear. It was the wettest, sloppiest, grossest thing in the world. He had a tongue that wouldn't stop. It wasn't just in my mouth; it was a wet kiss everywhere. I remember thinking, *This is kissing? How is this enjoyable?* We were in there for twenty or thirty minutes. Then the next time I was with a cute boy and I thought he might kiss me, I was, like, *okay, I've done it before,* and I kissed him without being as scared. I also found out (much to my relief) that the way Mark kissed me wasn't the norm. —Kim, Harrison, New York

Ending

In the beginning of the movie *Never Been Kissed*, Drew Barrymore's character, Josie, says that she has been kissed BUT not the kind that makes everything go hazy, where the only things in focus are her and the guy she's kissing. She goes on about the kind of kiss where she'll know at that moment that she'll be kissing him, and only him, for the rest of her life. Well, her friend laughed, called her a dreamer, and reminded her that she might have to kiss a lot of losers before she gets *that* kiss.

But that *doesn't* mean that kissing those boys (whether they are actually losers, or just not exactly Mr. Right) was a worthless activity, or a waste of her time. You can get closer to someone by kissing him, and in the process of kissing lots of frogs, you also learn a lot about yourself. Each kiss is an adventure, a possibility, a new door that could open. So, happy journeys, and may all your kisses be sweet!